A
LOVE THAT
TRANSFORMS

Leaving People better off than
you found them.

KEVIN J. RAY

Table of Contents

———————♦———————

Acknowledgments.. 1

Foreword 3

I didn't always do this right... 7

Know thyself.…… 12

Healthy to Explore… 19

Worth the Investment….. 32

Partnering up for the Mission… 37

This one is for you... 42

Acknowledgments

———◆———

This just a big shout out to those who helped me along the journey. I wanna start by thanking Kantrice Thomas from Birmingham, AL who encouraged me to write a book. Your seed of encouragement propelled me to start brainstorming. To my Aunt Jycnthia Moore and cousin Joshua Bailey who helped me battle for the best product possible. You two were honest and didn't hold back. I say this all the time Everyone needs a Aunt J in their life. Anybody who knows me knows the impact my aunties have had on my life. No matter how high I get I'm taking you with me because I know you coming with the raw honest loving truth. You're always helping me to become the best version of myself. Josh you put some

1

fire under me and held me accountable. Thank you I also want to thank Mrs. Yolaine Joseph-Sykes for editing my book. You've been a friend and mentor to me since P.D. Jackson Olin High School days. Thank you to Mrs. Angela Abdur-Rasheed for your constant encouragement. It's an honor to serve with you at our Church. Cherinita Reese you're the best! Thank you for your constant wisdom and prayers at every season. Thank you also to the amazing women that have been in my life that developed my stories and I pray God's best over your life.

Foreword

———◆———

My introduction to Kevin Ray's work "A Love That Transforms: Leaving people better off than you found them came in late September of 2018. His love and concern for relationships is a passion that we share and it has inspired me to start writing my own book. He's allowed me to mentor him for the past 6 years and I am so proud of the young man that he has become today. The book gives you insight on how to fight for the ones we often take for granted. Kevin's unorthodox approach to relationships is refreshing and it will help us to care for others well, as we learn to care for ourselves first. Kevin's heart beat is to see people walk in their purpose, the local church strengthened, and stronger unified families. It's all here. Honest expression, serious purpose, and playfulness all in one. There is no doubt that for Kevin, writing this book was a labor of love. For you, I hope reading it will be as well.

Jcynthia Moore, *Friend*

I remember it just like it was yesterday. A young big headed, tall, lanky, and brown boy from Ensley that struggled with insecurity, doubting himself, and had felt like he had no real voice. Thank you to transformational love that was a God send from my mama Patricia Ray, Aunt Brenda Bailey, Grandmother Hazel Bailey, Brother Larry Scott, Niel Parker and Aunt Jycnthia Moore. I recognize and honor those people because I can only imagine what life would have been like if neither of them stepped into my life. I'm from the Pittsburg of the south-Birmingham, AL where there is a church on every corner. The best hot lemon pepper wings you ever had. It's a cool balance that you can be slow when you want and fast when you want. I describe the people as beautiful, loyal, creative, and the sweetest people you'll ever meet. I grew up in a community in the Western side of town called Ensley. The statistics were against me. What stereotypes said about people who grew up in Ensley were against me. I came to realize, though the power of choosing people in your life, whose love and support empowered me which served as a weapon against the statistics or what society expected me to measure up too. Thank you for aiding my arsenal!

I didn't always do this right...

———◆———

It was December 14, 2014. I transgressed. I was leaving a girl's house in the morning and headed to my church. (As my grandma used to say "you going to get the guilt off ya"...Grandma knew the truth, God bless her sprit in Heaven). My Pastor spoke a word in season that sticks with me today, "Many times we feel lonely because we expect people to meet the needs that only God can meet." Little did I know the test was coming that day? I was in a five-year relationship. It was a great sales day. I called my then girlfriend at the time and she said," Kevin I need to talk to you... I don't feel at peace about us going forward with marriage or this relationship." You know how when you're hearing something at first; you kind of have to process what's being said, but when she hung up it sunk in. It sunk in that I lost my very best friend. I lost a girl that prayed for me, challenged me, traveled with me, cooked for me, loved my family, and showed me how much she loved me with so much detail. Not immediate but soon God would reveal to me "you don't deserve my daughter and I broke y'all up..." She had no proof of what I did, but her inner peace was troubled by God. Ladies that's a word. Like my homeboy Clinton Catlin so eloquently stated, "you can't run game on a woman who double checks with God about everything!!" It can't get no realer than that. Let me be transparent and clarify things before you start reading; I didn't always do this right and probably even make mistakes currently. I'm so thankful that God's mercies are new every morning. But to be honest I've taken advantage of other's kindness, had sex out of wedlock, and approached women I wasn't ready for or really interested in, and even cheated on a girl that was FOR me. She transformed my life. Taught me the importance of financial stewardship, propelled me even further in my walk with God, challenged me in traveling to new places, and genuinely always believed in my dreams. Gratefully we're still friends today, but God whispered to me, "she's my daughter and you won't mess over her". I never felt so much pain. In 2014 of December I was contemplating suicide after she told me that she didn't have any real peace about us moving forward towards our goals of being married. Thank God I had mentors, friends, worship music, and God Himself to pull me through. I respect the profession of mental health and encourage family and friends to get the help they need. I'm just a witness for me. I poured my heart out to God. I mean I let it rip on Him. I was cussing. I was hitting my bed. I was vulnerable in worship. I spoke his word over me, even when the lies of the enemy were very loud. I had genuine prayer warriors praying for me and reaching out to me. I share this to say that this is one of many scenarios that motivated me to share with others my heart to appreciate rare people. Yes, I truly believe some people are "once in a lifetime" type of people. There is no upgrade after them. In this book I hope to inspire you to appreciate them, but more importantly I pray you become one of them. I heard Dr. John Maxwell in a conference once say, "We attract who we are; not what we want." Let's make sure transformation love is in us first before we launch out in this very selfish world. Through this book we're going to explore the four steps of what I think every person whether Single, Satisfied, or Married should go through to experience fulfilling life giving transformative relationships. I won't hold back at all. No one is safe; not even me lol. I'm truly going to pour my heart and soul into this book. I also want to recommend books like Five Love languages by Gary Chapman, RelationTIPS by Life coach Anthony D. Sparks, Love and respect by Dr. Emerson and Eggerichs just in case you want to go deeper in relationships. Hey, be honest with me okay? I'm not really trying to sell a book, but I'm going to sell a book though. Feel me? I make this point to help you understand I'm not here to impress you; I'm actually here to help. Do you miss yourself? The person you were before you had your first heartbreak or before you got betrayed by a person you trusted? God wants to restore that person. Give me a blank page. Come into this with an open mind, an open heart, and then we're ready to take off friend! God I'm aware of the condition our generation is in. Some are in Deep pain, disappointment, disillusionment, fearful of starting over, feeling stuck and Lord I pray you bless the reader. Heal their heart, give them peace, clarity where there's confusion, give them courage to let go of what's draining and behold what's needful. In Jesus Name Amen. Let's get to work ya'll! Love you to life!

Know thyself......

———•◆•———

I believe we live in a dating culture whereas many people spend too much time dating others, but fail to "date" themselves. This is the time to be totally selfish. I've heard successful couples often say they waited to give themselves permission to date. I love that. If you really own this stage of life; I indeed think it's possible to not even want to go to the next steps of dating, because it's not hard to relish in this stage of knowing thyself. I want you to give yourself patience, grace, kindness, and truth. Invest in yourself. Read books, attend life giving churches, travel, exercise, take yourself out to dinners, and entertainment. You'd be surprised at how people think I'm weird because I take myself out on dates. I take good care of myself. On my days off it's not uncommon to catch me at a park, working out, eating my favorite soul food, getting my hair cut, or getting a spa massage. Study yourself because this is the time to get intimate with you, so you can properly discern your voice, what you like, and what you don't like. Only those who love themselves can love others well. Let me also recommend having mentors outside of your parents or family. You need people in your life who are not impressed with you, but love you. Solicit people that have your permission to ask the hard questions without you being offended. Everyone needs a mentor. I personally have five mentors and they all serve me in different ways. One can be for finances, family relations, personal goals, and ambitions. Life is just better when you can pour out what you wrestle with on your heart to people that won't judge you and will correct you lovingly. This is also a time where you should recognize your traumas and triggers. How aware are you of your traumas and suppressed emotions and tell me about how you are actively working to heal them? I grew up as a baby of four. (Shout out to my two sisters and big brother) My trauma is overthinking. Yes, I'm the guy who will double text. (Meaning I will keep checking on you to make sure we're good if the conversation is being delayed.) I don't know, but maybe it traces back to me being the baby of the family and always concerned about the general welfare of the family. They'll tell you I'm the one that calls everyone to check on them and their kids. I hate when the family is at war. It bothers me when they are not speaking to each other. I'm like really? You're not going to speak to your sister? I've just demonstrated my trauma here, but If not managed properly though I can come off worrisome, obsessive, and controlling. I've confronted this with practicing more patience and exploring different meditations through apps like "Calm" and "Head space". Now one of my triggers which is affection is a result that I also grew up in a single parent home. My mom was not very affectionate towards me and at times could be verbally abusive. Affection and affirmation are actually two of my love languages. Triggers can steam from what you've lacked in your upbringing as a child. Take for example let's just say you were always overlooked and didn't get to express yourself as much at the dinner table. Your parents often sought the opinion of your siblings over yours and that formed as a personal void. So when someone comes along and actually takes the time to listen to you; your love language of attention is being met by what you lacked growing up. I'll give you another example. Say growing up you never had anyone to take initiative, buy you nice things, or give you exposure to different experiences. Now your draw to anybody is them buying you nice things and taking you places. I would recommend reading the book Five Love Languages by Gary Chapman who masterfully details everyone's need for affirmation, physical touch, quality time, receiving gifts, or acts of service. It's important to recognize how you like to be loved. Me and my mom (to date) have a beautiful relationship. I love and pray for that woman every day. She's truly a different woman than who I grew up with. One of my chief prayer warriors, active in her church, and will just keep it real with you about where you stand and where you need to go. She did the best she could working two to three different jobs to provide for four bad ass kids. Being a single parent means your kids could be lacking things that kids from healthy homes do not. This is not a put down, but just letting you in on my reality a bit. Cause if I'm not careful this trigger can be exploited by another person. They may be toxic in other areas of their lives which could be detrimental to my purpose and mental health. I encourage you to write these two headings down on a note pad and list your **triggers** and **traumas**. I want also for you to list your **values** and **non-negotiables**. If you don't know who you are; now is a good time to find out. If you don't; you'll be subject to every "wave" culture throws your way. I recommend taking self-discovery classes, exploring 16personalities.com website, digging deep into your family history, and values etc. I'm genuinely praying this generation be a generation of principles and not ever changing unreliable opinions. Culture will always shift, it doesn't mean you have to. Some of my values are: a relationship with God through Jesus, commitment to family, love for people, being an advocate for the ones that don't have a voice just to name a few. My non-negotiables are: disrespect of any kind, not dating unbelievers who don't have a relationship with God, etc. My Aunt J says it beautifully," we gotta know who's ministry and who to partner with." Everyone deserves ministry, but not everyone deserves to partner with me. We gotta stop falling for people we were only supposed to help. Reader you should be literally living your best life and studying yourself with your best intentions. Get your finances in order, work on your mental healing, deal with those issues that keep showing up in every past relationship. I always ask women I'm considering dating, "What you learned in your last relationship? Don't just pack it up and keep jumping into relationships. What patterns keep showing up? Please use this valuable time to be hard on yourself and confront your reality. If you don't tell nobody else the truth;

tell yourself the truth! STOP dating while you're healing. You're damaging innocent people. Confused people confuse people. Hurting people hurt people. Wounded people wound people. Broken people break people. Bound people bind people. Damaged people damage people. Only healthy people help people.

Healthy to Explore...

———◆———

This stage is healthy once you've fully loved yourself in *know thy self.* Please don't take another step into this stage until you've honestly, carefully, and passionately loved yourself. Explore is fun because now you've raised the bar on what you can choose. Yes Sir, Yes mam you unfortunately can't choose your family (family shade lol I'm just being serious nah just joking I love my folks), but you can choose your friends/companion. You get to choose what type of life you want to build. You don't have to make the same mistakes your parents made, your friends, or what everyone else is making. Get excited! I'm just being serious. Now get excited!! Okay so I'm against women "shooting their shot". Side note: Women if you shoot your shot, you might just end up playing basketball by yourself while he's on the bench just looking at you put in all the work. Ladies should never shoot their shot. Just chill if he wants you, he'll work to get you. (He who finds a wife. Not SHE who shoots her shot.)I'm against women trying to vie for a man's attention. I really believe we as men are built for rejection. If a guy can't handle rejection like a mature man, it just shows how insecure and unconfident he really is and no woman should have to put up with that. That's really a warning sign that he needs to go back to *know thyself.* I've had women decline me or ignore me in the DMs and I respectfully withdrew my approach if it was a clear I'm uninterested. Meaning I'm getting no real tangible response. Now some women will create safeguard barriers primarily based on past experiences just to see how bad you really want it and that's ok. You're a man so if you pick up that the thirst is mutually there and she just playing cat and mouse. I want you to still be witty! Still be persistent! Now Men let me say this we're getting too old to be "shooting our shot", making the team, and then stop coming to practice. I know our generation has made it cool to not genuinely care anymore. We rather text than call. We call checking on you by checking your Facebook page or responding to posts. It's okay to be old fashioned. Shout out to the women that love conversations instead of "wyd" all the time! I don't want a relationship unless the thirst is mutual. I don't know about you I want someone matching my energy. *Mutual Reciprocity* will be a key throughout this book.

Age is just a number. Maturity is a choice. If we want to embrace transformational love; we must embrace growth. I'm convinced we live in a generation that prides itself on who can be the most childish. Always check for the ones that are expanding your thinking whether they're introducing you to books, genuinely consistently reaching out to attend different seminars, or even sending you podcasts to listen too. Those are the ones that understand the importance of fine tuning one's mind. Those are the ones that understand Self-reflection is essential for cleansing in order to remove whatever is hindering your own personal growth. They are not perfect, but they are very self-aware. Self-awareness is extremely attractive by the way. I like the word *self-actualization*. It's a word my Professor at Lawson State Community College Shelly Millender introduced me to. It's something I strive for daily. Psychologist Abraham Maslow outlines what is known as a hierarchy of needs, representing all the various needs that motivate human behavior. The hierarchy is often displayed as a pyramid, with the lowest levels representing basic needs and more complex needs located at the top of the pyramid. Self-actualized people accept themselves and others as they are. They tend to lack inhibition and are able to enjoy themselves and their lives free of guilt.

Not only do self-actualized people fully accept themselves, they also embrace other people for who they are. Other individuals are treated the same regardless of background, current status, or other socio-economic and cultural factors. In this age of social media; know that **many will fall in love with the idea of you, but very few will fall in love with the commitment of bettering your reality.** Maturity is realizing that there's no better feeling than being around someone who actually accepts your reality, loves & cares about the details of your life. Maturity is realizing and accepting that *you* may just be the problem. Second step...What are you going to do to fix it? Maturity is realizing that what's popular and under the surface are two different things. If they couldn't stand with you in the pit, they should not be able to serve with you in the palace. Connect with someone that realizes and works towards your potential. My good friend Bria says, "You never know someone til you know their dreams". Pay attention when they ask you about your life's mission, what breaks your heart so much that you want to make a difference about it, what keeps you up at night, and how can I come alongside and partner with you in making it happen. Yes Sir, Yes Mam, partnership! Hey, be okay with the questions somebody is asking you that nobody has previously asked you. That's discovery. That's effort. Effort is attractive. Listen I'm not calling on you to be normal or to what everyone else is doing. Normal isn't working. (I.E. the divorce rate, the girl or man on your timeline that's always in a new relationship, this is the one for sure, and so on). I'm calling you to be effective and God desires for your partnership to be effective in blessing others. Don't break your own heart by assuming that person had the same intentions as you. Ask questions, see what they are looking for, what's their value/belief system and always pray about it. You can't just assume that person is God's will just because they show interest in you. Be intentional, because all of that "going with the flow" is going to lead you into a situation-ship that isn't heading towards God or marriage. A situationship is best defined by Urban Dictionary as a relationship that has no label on it... like a friendship but more than a friendship but not quite a relationship. Where one person leads another person on letting them think that the end product of their time together would amount to a relationship when in reality the individual only wanted an outlet for sex and a momentary emotional connection.

It literally amazes me when people start the dating process that they have no questions. Like for real no questions? Secure people should be able to handle your questions. Oh, don't worry ladies this is not one of those books where the author just focuses on women and tell them what they want to hear. We both men and women have work to do. Now I understand that some of my women friends like to say, "naw I'd rather look at your actions because that's going to tell me just what I need to know". I get that. Actions matter. I just don't want us getting away from the power of clarity, commitment, and affirming promises to each other. **Let's stop having relationship problems with somebody you aren't in a relationship with.** We can't lead off assumptions alone. Assumptions kill, but communication kills assumptions. Talk it out like grown adults. Boys will bring confusion & chaos.

A man who is about you wants to provide clarity & peace. But wait, you love your mystery prospect huh? Lol. A lotta women are just committing to boyfriends based off assumptions. Don't be fooled. It's a reason he's so quiet...you're the one calling the shots...he ain't said not a thing...why buy the cow when you can get the milk for free?(That's what the old folks used to say) All this "well we koolin" "long as me and him know what's up"..."what's understood don't need to be explained." You know all the cool innuendos we throw out there? Lol. Really then he gotchu where you ain't worth a public declaration of his love for you and intent to marry you? Lol. I been hanging around my grandma too much. Lawd I miss her!! Seriously though, if marriage is not the goal; then you're wasting precious time. Men by nature love a challenge, love a chase, and respect logistics up front for the woman their eyeing.

Men and women: when seeking a companion here's some questions to consider.

1. Do they love and fear God? Sure, everybody loves God but not everybody fears or respects His guidelines (His Word) for living. I'm not talking perfection here, but about someone who is honest about where they are and genuinely wants to grow. They want to be an example to their kids.

2. How does he respond when he loses something (I.E. Game, competition, a bet, etc.) if he punches a wall? That may be you one day ladies. How does she respond when she can't have her way? Really you can tell a lot about a person's character when the answer is no.

3. What do they laugh at? What do they find entertaining? If you find yourself sharing something very serious to you with them, one day you may not find it humorous. The lifestyle that they're embracing through music, television, or videos they share through social media may not reflect the lifestyle you actually want to live.

4. What's their core like? What are their values? What's their non-negotiables? What are their relationships like with their parents? How do they view men and view women?

Fella's conversation is everything. I was fortunate to be raised around strong women who helped me learn how to communicate effectively and understand women better. Women are so dope. Every person of the opposite sex that comes across your path doesn't have to be a romantic attraction. It's okay to just be friends. Some of us may just need healthy friendships. Embrace women friends, they can help sharpen your dialogue as well. If we stir a woman's deep emotions without a matching commitment, of course she seems "crazy". Commitment & intimacy must match. "Well Kev you know I'm a man of 'few words'. I hate it when she talking my ear off...." it's just an attitude. If you can go on and on with your homies about a team you don't know, then surely you can invest in the girl that's closest to you a good conversation. Better learn how to converse with your woman or someone else will form that mental connection that you're too "cool" to participate in. A local Rapper who was a friend of the family nicknamed Bam Bam once said, "fellas go with the woman who has her mind made up!". One mistake we do is **falling for people who we were only suppose to help.** How a person leads themselves is extremely attractive. No one is looking for another miscellaneous bill. How a person handles money should be more important than their salary. What are their priorities when spending money? Men don't lead with your money in this stage. Now I'm not saying don't do nice things for your love interest, but what I am saying is guard against being used. Get with someone who wants to love you, values your presence and enjoys the real not merely trying to use you. Men embrace the woman that encourages you, respects your vision and purpose, accepts and sees you for you, prays for you, values you getting closer to God, helps you *budget and grow your money* not just spend it on frivolous things and dining out. This is the person that's trying to elevate you. I know people have different situations, but I encourage you to look at the person's heart. The dates should be ones that stimulate conversation. Coffee dates, ice cream dates, walks in the parks, hiking, visiting museums and historical landmarks, picnics etc. These activities foster an atmosphere for someone trying to really get to know you without distractions. Movies, clubs, and places of entertainment really distract from the goal of being intimate without engaging in sex. If you're a virgin stay a virgin. Most of us who have crossed that line will tell you we regret losing our virginity and could have waited. If you're sexually active; I encourage you to makes efforts to abstain so you can see clearly and focus on who the person is in front of you. Participating in the latter of the activities such as entertainment comes later after you have determined that the chemistry and vibe between you is right. The early stages of dating should not be, "I'm here to entertain you" rather "I'm here to get to know you"... Study them. Pay attention to how they act around your friends and their friends.

Love cannot be learned in isolation. You have to be around people- irritating, imperfect, and frustrating people. Ask about their family history. Ask how they were raised. Take note: Do they ask you similar questions? Family dynamics are everything (Which will be my next book; shameless plug right?). **You should never have to shrink or hide who you are to make anyone comfortable.** If and when someone you're dating is trying to isolate you from your family and healthy friendships; just know you're in a dangerous toxic space. Users will isolate you from loved ones- much like an abuser would. This is because they want you to feel dependent on their love, attention, and because being alone makes you easier to manipulate. If there are more green checks than red flags you may have permission to go to the next step. Through this whole process I tell people you should be praying, "God show me their heart. Show me their character. Is this the one truly for me?"

Let's step on to investment because this is really where the rubber meets the road!

Worth the Investment...

———◆———

This is the stage where everything we've stated, spent, committed begins to match what we do. Love has corresponding actions. Love will always be sacrificial on both ends. People throw the word love around so easy, but they don't really know what it means. It's a deliberate, daily choice. It's not just something you say, it's something you do. It's inconvenient. It's sacrificial. It's more than just that butterfly feeling. Remember my good friend Bria told me," you never know a person until you know their dreams." In the previous step of exploring we should remember their dreams and do something tangible to invest in them. Whether it's support (some people just need us to show up, give them a book on their craft, or even purchase a tool that helps them focus on their craft. Nothing spells love then investing in what I do. Empowerment is the highest form of love to me. My ex-girlfriend purchased me a laptop for $500 and she was a college student. That was sacrifice on her part even when she didn't have a job. That computer helped me work with broadcast radio when I was attending Auburn University. It takes both the man and woman pouring into each other to build and experience a happy and fulfilling relationship.

There's someone out there building up your future spouse. Be happy that you're doing the same for someone else. Even if it hurts. We're all preparing each other for someone else. Let's make better men and women. Leave people better than you found them. So yes, be the guy that's invested books, paid for seminars for your love interest to attend, invest in her dreams, and tell her who she really is. Be the woman that's encouraging him, exposing him to activities he otherwise wouldn't have experienced without your nudging, or calling out his potential.

Our community desperately needs it, our future kids depend on it, and our world is looking for it. A love with no conditions and no agenda other than to build up truly is rewarding for both parties. I know what you are thinking, "But Kev I risk investing so much and might end up with the short stick". Author Bob Goff once said, "Loving people means caring without an agenda. As soon as we have an agenda, it's not love anymore." What goes around comes around. When you do good things for others without expecting anything in return, good things will come back to you! I truly believe God will have something good on the other end. Let me say though to the receiver. Your blinkers need to be on!! You telling me you overlooking somebody who has seen your reality and still says they'll commit to make it better? That's a keeper! That's somebody that wants better days for you. I like the story in Mark 12:41. "Jesus sat down opposite the place where the offerings were put and watched the crowd putting their money into the temple treasury. Many rich people threw in large amounts. 42 But a poor widow came and put in two very small copper coins, worth only a few cents.

43 Calling his disciples to him, Jesus said, "Truly I tell you, this poor widow has put more into the treasury than all the others. 44 They all gave out of their wealth; but she, out of her poverty, put in everything—all she had to live on." This illustrates what sacrificial love looks like. No, I'm not advocating that one should be poor or for struggle love. What I am saying is that if I'm rich the investment in a woman would be me investing in her empowerment. Write that rich man a business proposal and see if he'd invest in it. Anyone can sex you, feed you and buy you stuff, but it takes someone REAL and RARE that's interested in you to help you become the best version of yourself, invest in your craft, build, and work with you for a better LIFE. Pay attention to their heart y'all not their wallet. If their heart screams commitment and investing in you; go for it! It'll only go up from there! Culture trumps everything. Good soil is the key to growth. Recognize the difference between

someone who's adding to soil and someone who just shows up for the fruit. Sex is everywhere, but chemistry isn't. Sometimes we can get caught up in what we think we want to only overlook what we need. Be secure in something that's a good thing. Don't overlook a good thing for a good time. The good thing is what's going to be solid for the storms of life, the family crisis, the transitions in life, etc. A good time over time will be played out and moved on to the next new thing. I'm willing to bet you overlooked your best friend lol. Best Relationship: Talk like best friends, play like children, argue like husband and wife, and protect each other like brother and sister. Somebody you genuinely like being around. The best and most effective relationships are between best-friends. It's so lit. Stop second guessing yourself. Just imagine the effort you give times 2 reciprocated back to you I don't think you hear me... y'all would be something serious fore-real. Alright let's get on to the Mission!

Partnering up for the Mission...

————◆————

Y'all we are wrappin' up soon! This is my favorite part of the conversation. Because I think this is where people really miss it. If you successfully navigated the previous three steps then now is the time to really live your best life! Michelle Obama told her husband "the view is always better with you." Most couples fail because they have no mission attached to what they do. Every couple and family house hold needs a mission. Really, I would dare to say you need a mission individually. It is what will make you attractive. It is what will draw people to you. Honestly if you navigated these steps with a pure heart; you'll appreciate people that helped you with your mission. Cause guess what the people that weren't in the gym with you will more than likely only fall in love with your mission and not your reality. Everyone loves the mission. It's not by accident that God brought you two together. Look deep within to your core and your roots. See how you two complement each other in the grand scheme of things. God has a mission on your life. The people you're called to impact will in fact remind you two of why you're together. You're here to make a difference. And this isn't deep y'all, but I am challenging you to live and love deeply. Practically the mission can look like the two of you hosting marriage small group meetings to help others who face similar battles, mentoring the boys and girls in your neighborhoods, serving the local neighborhood school's football team, creating safe spaces for people to just love on. This mission is what's going to keep the ship afloat! It's going to solve petty arguments quicker too I bet. Lol. I can imagine the conversation going like, "baby we got to make up cause you know those kids are coming over." I dream of more mature love, because the next generation so desperately needs to see it demonstrated. I want to go back to the days of when families were known for something. For example, if somebody saw my future child; they'd probably be like, "oh she's a Ray" she comes from a family of writers. The two of you are a team for a reason! Honor his gift. Honor her gift. Affirm his gift. Affirm her gift. I want you to genuinely intercede far as praying for him and praying for her to be presented with more opportunities that point to them walking out their purpose. That's the ultimate fulfillment. It's cool to have long term safety net goals like getting a new house, retirement, and passing on generational wealth to your kids. Let me say this though, no one at your funeral is going to talk about how nice your car was or how big and spacious your house was. My sister and husband hosts kids in the neighborhood over to their house and let them play basketball. She feeds them. I said to her recently that's a ministry. We'll be known for our opinions but remembered by our love. What will people in your life line up at your funeral and thank you for? What are you leaving behind when you leave this world? Possessions will fade away and wear out, but a legacy of love will last into eternity. Please y'all, genuinely pray about your mission and have the guts to walk it out. Too many couples suffer from stagnation. That's why we got so many cheating couples. You have either two extremes. One is doing their purpose and the other is not, or worse both people doing nothing but going through the motions. You need transformative impactful goals for your marriage. How will God use you two to leave a mark on the world? I'm praying for business partnerships to be launched, collaborative books written, and small group meetings for other single people or couples debating divorce. You don't know what or who hangs in the balance of your obedience. I'm tired of so many boring, mundane, failed marriages, and worst disappointed kids who turn into angry adults. Please take the step. Someone is counting on your courage. Someone is counting on your innovation. All this I discussed was hard to do through merely will-power alone. So

I encourage you to pray this prayer with me sincerely. "God you are love. You don't have it; You are the source of love and Today I receive your transformational love that you demonstrated by sending your Son to die for me. Jesus change me. Love people through me and I'll never be the same. From this day forward I give you my life. In your name I pray Amen." Love you to life and I pray you walked away from this book not only inspired, but at least focused, intentional, and moved to action to build productive secure relationships. Blessings

This one is for you...

———◆———

Love people passionately, but hold them loosely. Men and Ladies this is a tough one but have some guts to ask it. I've had to do this in my past and even currently. Do yourself a favor and ask your significant other this question. "Do you love me enough to not get in my way concerning my growth in God and concerning my purpose in life?" Love them so much that you can let them go and fly even if you're not in the picture. Always pray for the best for someone even if it doesn't include you. That's what true love is. This is the epitome of selfless love. Be the type of person to leave people better off than you found them and pray that God sends other genuine people across their path to finish the journey. I suspect I know what you're thinking. Kev I can't do that. It's too risky. I might lose out investing in someone that may not feel as passionate about me. Let me tell you you reap what you sow. Good or bad my friend; the harvest of what one plants will come back. Can I tell you I stand confidently with the women I've pursued and say "there's more where that came from". (Lol confidence huh?) This Love is costly. This is my good stuff lol. You can't find this everywhere. Hey, you need to have the same attitude and be just as picky with who you give it to. Only smart people take note. And to you on the other end that may find it advantageous to take advantage of the kindness of people. This generation often makes the mistake of trading a "good thing" for a good time. You're losing out and need to grow up. It's not cute to just go around playing with people's emotions, money, peace of mind and hearts ... that's not "juice" ... that's just cold and childish .To pride yourself on being a finesser, a user, a manipulator?? What you send out, comes back. What you sow, you reap. What you give, you get. What you see in others, exists in you. Quit playing with people's emotions. Be honest about what you want or leave them alone. Don't break your own heart by assuming that person had the same intentions as you. Let me also say if we don't steward the life giving people that God gives us; we really risk going through life with life takers. Ask questions, see what they are looking for, and always pray about it. You can't just assume that person is God's will just because they show interest in you. Be intentional, because all of that "going with the flow" is going to lead you into another situation-ship that isn't heading towards God or marriage. If you don't have good intentions. Leave! And y'all wonder why all these domestic cases be happening?? Be careful it's real out here. My hope was that I was honest in who I am, the battles that I've faced, facing, etc. I pray you came away from this book encouraged, focused, more intentional, grateful, eyes opened, and hearts willing to love again. Thank you and I pray this book was a well spent investment and that it left you better off after you've read it.

Made in the USA
Monee, IL
12 October 2021